STEPS TO
FREEDOM
IN CHRIST

Neil Anderson titles published by Monarch Books:

The Bondage Breaker (Study Guide Edition)
Freedom from Fear
God's Power at Work in You
Victory Over the Darkness (Study Guide Edition)
Restored

Steve Goss titles published by Monarch Books:

Break Free, Stay Free
Free to be Yourself
Win the Daily Battle
The You God Planned

Available from Christian bookshops or from Freedom in Christ Ministries.

Dedication

This version of *Steps to Freedom in Christ* is dedicated to Clare Prichard with grateful thanks for her tireless commitment to seeing Christians in the UK set free to experience God's love, and for her enormous effort in helping churches get up and running with their own freedom ministries.

STEPS TO
FREEDOM
IN CHRIST

NEIL T.
ANDERSON

MONARCH
BOOKS
Oxford, UK & Grand Rapids, Michigan, USA

First published in the UK in 2000 by Monarch Books,
(a publishing imprint of Lion Hudson plc),
Wilkinson House, Jordan Hill Road, Oxford, OX2 8DR
Tel: +44 (0) 1865 302750   Fax: +44 (0) 1865 302757
monarch@lionhudson.com
www.lionhudson.com

Revised edition published in 2003.
Reprinted in 2004, 2006, 2007.
This revised edition published in 2009.

ISBN: 978-1-85424-943-2

Distributed by
Marston Book Services Ltd, PO Box 269, Abingdon, Oxon OX14 4YN

This book has been printed on paper and board independently
certified as having come from sustainable forests.

British Library Cataloguing Data
A catalogue record for this book is available
from the British Library.

Printed and bound in England by J F Print Ltd.

Contents

How To Get The Most From *The Steps To Freedom In Christ*

By Steve Goss, Director, Freedom In Christ Ministries (UK)

The Steps To Freedom In Christ is a wonderfully refreshing process for *every* Christian. I try to go through it once a year as a kind of spiritual check-up and find it hugely beneficial. It clears away the spiritual cobwebs and helps me connect with Jesus.

It also works well if you are facing particular challenges. If you seem to be going round in circles as a Christian, if you sense that you are simply not growing as you should be, if you struggle in your thought life, or if you are stuck in a cycle of sin-confess-sin-confess that you can't seem to break, then *The Steps To Freedom In Christ* can help.

It's always a delight to receive comments such as these from people who have used the Steps:

"I can truly say that, after finding Jesus as my Saviour, entering into the fullness of my spiritual freedom in Christ has been the most significant moment of my life – I recommend it."

"The release that I felt at years of shame and bondage being lifted from me is hard to describe. I really do not know what to say – I feel like a human being again!"

"My life has been transformed. It truly was like walking from darkness back into light again."

"I have a clear head, praise Jesus – it's not been really clear for years!"

"Finding my freedom in Christ has changed my life."

This is no "magic formula", no zany self-help product – it's pure biblical truth in a very helpful package. After all, it's not the Steps that set you free – it's Jesus Christ.

To get the full benefit you'll need to be prepared to do some work. If you are serious about claiming the freedom that Christ has already won for you, and want to avoid falling back into unproductive ways of thinking, it's essential that you take time to understand what the Bible says about who you are in Christ.

The best way I know to do this is to go through The Freedom In Christ Discipleship Course, ideally in your own church. Alternatively, you can get the teaching by reading Neil Anderson's main books, *Victory Over The Darkness* and *The Bondage Breaker*, or the Discipleship Series of books that I wrote to accompany the Discipleship Course (read them before you go through the Steps and again afterwards). There are further details at the back of this book on page 96.

The Steps To Freedom In Christ

Getting Started

"It was for freedom that Christ set us free; therefore keep standing firm and do not be subject again to a yoke of slavery" (Galatians 5:1). If you have received Christ as your Saviour, He has already set you free through His victory over sin and death on the cross. The question is: "Are you living victoriously in Christ's freedom or are you living in bondage, however subtle or strong?"

Christ offers you freedom from personal and spiritual conflicts, freedom from sin and the negative programming of your past, freedom from the damaging effects of guilt and unforgiveness. Freedom opens the pathway to knowing, loving, worshipping and obeying God. It is the joyful experience of living by faith according to what God says is true and in the power of the Holy Spirit, and it means not carrying out the desires of the flesh. It doesn't mean perfection, but it is a growing and abundant life in Christ who alone can meet our deepest needs for life, identity, acceptance, security and significance.

Regaining Your Freedom

If you are not experiencing this life of freedom, it may be because you have not stood firm in the faith or lived according to who you are in Christ. Somehow you have returned again to a yoke of slavery (see Galatians 5:1). Your eternal destiny is not at stake, but your daily victory is.

No matter how difficult your life might be, there is great news for you. You are not a helpless victim caught between two nearly equal but opposite heavenly superpowers. Satan is a liar and a deceiver, and the only way he can have power over you is if you believe his lies.

Only God is all-powerful, always present and all-knowing. Sometimes the reality of sin and the presence of evil may seem more real than the presence of God, but that's part of Satan's deception. Satan is a defeated foe and we are alive in Christ.

The Steps to Freedom in Christ do not set you free. *Who* sets you free is Christ; *what* sets you free is your response to Him in repentance and faith. The Steps provide an opportunity for you to have an encounter with God, the Wonderful Counsellor, by submitting to Him and resisting the devil (see James 4:7). They are a means of resolving personal and spiritual conflicts that have kept you from experiencing the freedom and victory Christ purchased for you on the cross. Your freedom will be the result of what *you* choose to believe, confess, forgive, renounce and forsake. No one can do that for you.

The Battle for Your Mind

There is a battle going on for your mind, which is the control centre of all that you think and do. The opposing thoughts you may experience as you go through these Steps can affect you only if you believe them. You may have nagging thoughts like, *"This isn't going to work"*, or *"God doesn't love me"*. Don't believe Satan's deceptions; don't pay any attention to accusing or threatening thoughts.

The battle for your mind can only be won as you personally choose truth. As you go through the process, remember that Satan is under no obligation to obey your thoughts. Only God has complete knowledge of your mind because He alone is all-knowing. Find a private place where you can say each Step out loud. You can submit to God inwardly, but you need to resist the devil by saying each prayer, declaration, etc aloud.

These Steps address critical issues between you and

God. It is possible to go through them on your own because Jesus is the Wonderful Counsellor, but many find it helps significantly to be led through by someone else, especially if there are deeper issues. The best environment for most people to go through the Steps is in the context of a local church which has people trained to encourage you and help you stand firm afterwards. Freedom In Christ Ministries may be able to refer you to a local church with a freedom ministry, but in the first instance why not ask your pastor for advice.

Both gaining and maintaining your freedom will be greatly enhanced if you first read *Victory Over the Darkness* and *The Bondage Breaker*. They will help you further understand the reality of the spiritual world and your relationship to it. While these Steps can play a major role in your continuing process of discipleship, there is no such thing as instant maturity. Renewing your mind and conforming to the image of God is a life-long process.

Regardless of the source of any difficulty you may have, you have nothing to lose and possibly everything to gain by praying through these issues. If you face problems that seem to stem from a source other than those covered in these Steps, you may need to seek professional help. (Consult a pastor or other trusted Christian leader for help in choosing the right professional.) The real focus here is your relationship with God. The lack of resolution of any one of these issues will affect your intimacy with Him and your daily victory in Christ.

Trust God to Lead You

Each Step is explained so you will have no problem knowing what to do. It doesn't make any difference whether or not there are evil spirits present; God is always present. If you experience any resistance, stop and pray. If you experience some mental opposition, just ignore it. It is just a thought, and it can have no power over you unless you believe it. Throughout the process, you will be asking God to lead you. He is the One who grants repentance leading to a knowledge of the truth that sets you free (see 2 Timothy 2:24–26). Begin the Steps with the following prayer and declaration. (If you are going through them on your own, change "we" to "I", and so on.)

May the Lord bless and guide you as you go through these Steps. Then, having found your freedom in Christ, you can help others experience the joy of their salvation.

Prayer

Dear Heavenly Father,
We acknowledge Your presence in this room and in our lives. You are the only all-knowing, all-powerful and ever-present God. We are dependent upon You, for apart from You we can do nothing. We stand in the truth that all authority in heaven and on earth has been given to the resurrected Christ, and because we are in Christ, we share that authority in order to make disciples and set captives free. We ask You to fill us with Your Holy Spirit and lead us into all truth. We pray for Your complete protection and ask for Your guidance. In Jesus' name. Amen.

Declaration

In the name and authority of the Lord Jesus Christ, we command Satan and all evil spirits to release _____ (name) in order that _____ (name) can be free to know and choose to do the will of God. As children of God seated with Christ in the heavenly places, we agree that every enemy of the Lord Jesus Christ be bound to silence. We say to Satan and all your evil workers that you cannot inflict any pain or in any way prevent God's will from being accomplished in _____ (name's) life. _____ (name) belongs to God and the evil one cannot touch him/her.

Preparation

Before going through the Steps to Freedom, review the events of your life to discern specific areas that might need to be addressed.

Family History

— Religious history of parents and grandparents

— Home life from childhood through to secondary school

— History of physical or emotional illness in the family

— Adoption, foster care, guardians

Personal History

— Eating habits (bulimia, bingeing and purging, anorexia, compulsive eating)

— Addictions (drugs, alcohol)

— Prescription medications (what for?)

— Sleeping patterns and nightmares

— Rape or any other sexual, physical, emotional abuse

— Thought life (obsessive, blasphemous, condemning, distracting thoughts, poor concentration, fantasy)

— Mental interference during church, prayer or Bible study
Emotional life (anger,

___ anxiety, depression,
bitterness, fears)

Spiritual journey
___ (salvation: when, how and
assurance)

Now you are ready to begin. The following are seven specific Steps to process in order to experience freedom from your past. You will address the areas where Satan most commonly takes advantage of us because strongholds have been built.

If your problems stem from a source other than those covered in these Steps, you have nothing to lose by going through them. If you are sincere, the only thing that can happen is that you will get right with God!

Step 1
Counterfeit versus Real

The first Step towards experiencing your freedom in Christ is to renounce (verbally reject) all past or present involvement with occult practices, cult teachings and rituals, as well as non-Christian religions.

You must renounce any activity or group which denies Jesus Christ or offers guidance through any source other than the absolute authority of the Bible. Any group that requires secret initiations, ceremonies, promises or pacts should also be renounced. Begin this step by praying aloud:

Dear Heavenly Father,
I ask You to bring to my mind anything and everything that I have done, knowingly or unknowingly, that involves occult, cult or non-Christian teachings or practices. I want to experience Your freedom by renouncing all counterfeit teachings and practices. In Jesus' name. Amen.

Even if you took part in something and thought it was just a game or a joke, you need to renounce it. Satan will try to take advantage of anything he can in our lives, so it is always wise to be as thorough as possible. Even if you were just standing by and watching others do it, you need to renounce your passive involvement. You may not have even realised at the time that what was going on was evil. Still, go ahead and renounce it.

If something comes to your mind and you are not sure what to do about it, trust that the Spirit of God is answering your prayer, and renounce it.

The following "Non-Christian Spiritual Experience Inventory" covers many of the more common occult, cult, and non-Christian religious groups and practices. It is not a complete list, however. Feel free to add others that you were personally involved with.

After the checklist, there are some additional questions designed to help you become aware of other things you may need to renounce. Below those questions is a short prayer of confession and renunciation. Pray it aloud, filling in the blanks with the groups, teachings, or practices that the Holy Spirit has prompted you to renounce during this time of personal evaluation.

Non-Christian Spiritual Experience Inventory

(Tick all those that you have participated in)

OCCULT
- ❑ Out-of-body experience (astral projection)
- ❑ Ouija board
- ❑ Bloody Mary
- ❑ Light as a feather (or other occult games)
- ❑ Table or body lifting
- ❑ Magic Eight Ball
- ❑ Spells or curses
- ❑ Mental telepathy or mental control of others
- ❑ ESP (Extra sensory perception)
- ❑ Automatic writing
- ❑ Trances
- ❑ Spirit guides
- ❑ Fortune telling/ divination (e.g. tea leaves)
- ❑ Tarot cards
- ❑ Levitation
- ❑ Magic – The Gathering
- ❑ Materialisation
- ❑ Clairvoyance
- ❑ Visualisation/ guided imagery
- ❑ Rod/pendulum (dowsing)
- ❑ Witchcraft/ Wicca/sorcery
- ❑ Satanism
- ❑ Palm reading

- [ ] Astrology/ horoscopes
- [ ] Hypnosis
- [ ] Séances
- [ ] Black or White magic
- [ ] Fantasy games with occult images
- [ ] Blood pacts or cutting yourself on purpose
- [ ] Objects of worship/ crystals/good luck charms
- [ ] Sexual spirits
- [ ] Martial arts (mysticism/ devotion to sensei)
- [ ] Superstitions (touching wood, salt over shoulder, Friday 13th)
- [ ] Fetishes
- [ ] Voodoo
- [ ] Spells and incantations
- [ ] Occult or violent video or computer games

OTHER RELIGIONS
- [ ] Buddhism (including Zen)
- [ ] Hinduism
- [ ] Islam
- [ ] Black Muslim
- [ ] Yoga
- [ ] Hare Krishna
- [ ] Silva Mind Control
- [ ] Bahai faith
- [ ] Rosicrucianism
- [ ] Ancestor worship
- [ ] Worshipping tribal deities (name them)
- [ ] Other non-Christian religions or cults

CULTS, etc.
- [ ] Mormonism (Latter-day Saints)
- [ ] Jehovah's Witnesses
- [ ] Masons
- [ ] Christadelphians
- [ ] Christian Science
- [ ] Mind Science cults
- [ ] The Way International
- [ ] Unification Church (Moonies)
- [ ] The Forum (EST)
- [ ] Children of God (Children of Love)
- [ ] Church of Scientology
- [ ] Unitarianism/ Universalism
- [ ] Transcendental Meditation (TM)
- [ ] New Age (books, objects, seminars, medicine)
- [ ] Feng Shui
- [ ] Reiki

List films, TV shows, music, books, magazines, or comics that the Lord is bringing to your mind (especially those that glorified Satan, caused fear or nightmares, were gruesomely violent, or stimulated the flesh).

_____

_____

The following questions are designed to help you become aware of other things you may need to renounce.

1. Have you ever seen, heard or felt a spiritual being in your room?

   _____

   _____

2. Do you have recurring nightmares? Specifically renounce any accompanying fear.

   _____

   _____

3. Do you have, or have you ever had, an imaginary friend, spirit guide or "angel" offering you guidance or companionship? (If it has a name, renounce it by name.)

   _____

   _____

4. Have you ever heard voices in your head or had repeating, nagging thoughts such as *I'm stupid, I'm ugly, nobody loves me, I can't do anything right* – as if there were a conversation going on inside your head? List any specific nagging thoughts and renounce them using the special prayer after question nine (p.20).

   _____

   _____

5. Have you ever consulted a medium, spiritualist, or channeller?

   _____

   _____

6. Have you ever seen or been contacted by beings you thought were aliens?

_____

_____

7. Have you ever made a secret vow or pact (or inner vow, e.g. *I will never...*)?

_____

_____

8. Have you ever been involved in a satanic ritual of any kind or attended a concert in which Satan was the focus?

_____

_____

9. What other spiritual experiences have you had that were evil, confusing or frightening?

_____

_____

Once you have completed your checklist and the questions, confess and renounce each item you were involved in by praying the following prayer aloud:

Lord Jesus,
I confess that I have participated in _____
(activity), and I renounce _____
(activity) and cancel out any effect the enemy gained in my life. Thank You that in Christ I am forgiven. Amen.

Special prayer for question 4 to renounce repeating, nagging thoughts:

Lord Jesus,
I confess I have paid attention to the voices or thoughts in my mind of _____, *and believed*

those repeating, nagging and condemning messages as though a dialogue was going on in my head. They were foreign to what I now choose to believe. I ask Your forgiveness, and I renounce paying attention to those voices or thoughts in my mind, and giving in to the dialogue in my mind. Amen.

When you have finished confessing and renouncing each item, pray the following prayer:

Lord,
I confess I have participated in these wrongful practices. I know they were evil and offensive in Your sight. Thank You for Your forgiveness. I renounce any and all involvement in these wrongful practices, and I choose to believe that Satan no longer has any rightful place in my life because of those involvements. In Jesus' name. Amen.

Evaluate Your Priorities

We were created to worship the true and living God. The Father seeks those who will worship Him in spirit and in truth (see John 4:23). As children of God, "We know also that the Son of God has come and has given us understanding, so that we may know Him who is true. And we are in Him who is true – even in His Son Jesus Christ. He is the true God and eternal life" (1 John 5:20, NIV).

The apostle John follows the above passage with a warning: "Little children, guard yourselves from idols" (1 John 5:21). An idol is a false god, any object of worship other than the true God. Though we may not bow down to statues, it is easy for people and things of this world subtly to become more important to us than our relationship with God. The following prayer expresses the commitment of a heart that chooses to "worship the Lord your God, and serve Him only" (Matthew 4:10).

Dear Lord God,

I know how easy it is to allow other things and other people to become more important to me than You. I also know that this is offensive to Your holy eyes as You have commanded that I should have no other gods before You.

I confess to You that I have not loved You with all my heart and soul and mind. As a result, I have sinned against You, violating the first and greatest commandment. I repent of and turn away from this idolatry and now choose to return to You, Lord Jesus, as my first love.

Please reveal to my mind any and all idols in my life. I choose to renounce every idol that would give Satan any right in my life. In the name of Jesus, the true God. Amen.

(See Exodus 20:3; Matthew 22:37; Revelation 2:4,5.)

The checklist below may help you recognise those areas where things or people have become more important to you than the true God, Jesus Christ. Notice that most (if not all) of the areas listed below are not evil in themselves; they become idols when they take God's rightful place as Lord of our lives.

- ❏ Ambition
- ❏ Food or any substance
- ❏ Money/possessions
- ❏ Computers/games/software
- ❏ Financial security
- ❏ Rock stars/media celebrities/athletes
- ❏ Church activities
- ❏ TV/films/music/other media
- ❏ Sports or physical fitness
- ❏ Fun/pleasure
- ❏ Ministry
- ❏ Appearance/image
- ❏ Work
- ❏ Busyness/activity
- ❏ Friends
- ❏ Power/control
- ❏ Boyfriend/girlfriend
- ❏ Popularity/opinion of others
- ❏ Spouse
- ❏ Knowledge/being right
- ❏ Children
- ❏ Hobbies
- ❏ Parents
- ❏ Others:

Use the following prayer to renounce any areas of idolatry or wrong priority the Holy Spirit brings to your mind:

Lord, I confess that I have made _____ *(person or thing) more important than You and I renounce that false worship. I choose to worship only You, Lord. I ask You, Father, to enable me to keep this area of* _____ *(name the idol) in its proper place in my life. In Jesus' name. Amen.*

Satanic Rituals or Heavy Occult Activity

If you have been involved in satanic rituals or heavy occult activity or you suspect it because of blocked memories, severe and recurring nightmares, or sexual bondage or dysfunction, we strongly urge you to say aloud these special renunciations for satanic ritual involvement. Read across the page, renouncing the first item in the column under Kingdom of Darkness and then announcing the first truth in the column under Kingdom of Light. Continue down the page in that manner.

Some people who have been subjected to Satanic Ritual Abuse (SRA) develop multiple or alternate personalities in order to cope with their pain. If this is true in your case, you need someone who understands spiritual conflict to help you work through this problem. For now, walk through the rest of the Steps to Freedom in Christ as best you can. It is important that you remove any demonic strongholds in your life before trying to integrate the personalities. Every personality that surfaces must be acknowledged and guided into resolving his or her issues. Then, all true personalities can agree to come together in Christ.

Special Renunciations

Kingdom of Darkness	Kingdom of Light
I renounce ever signing my name over to Satan or having my name signed over to Satan.	I announce that my name is now written in the Lamb's Book of Life.
I renounce any ritual where I was wed to Satan.	I announce that I am the Bride of Christ.
I renounce any and all covenants, agreements or promises that I have made to Satan.	I announce that I have made a new covenant with Christ.
I renounce all satanic assignments for my life, including duties, marriage and children.	I announce and commit myself to know and do only the will of God and I accept only His guidance for my life.
I renounce all spirit guides assigned to me.	I announce and accept only the leading of the Holy Spirit.
I renounce ever giving of my blood in the service of Satan.	I trust only in the shed blood of my Lord Jesus Christ.
I renounce ever eating of flesh or drinking of blood for satanic worship.	By faith I take Holy Communion which represents the body and the blood of the Lord Jesus.
I renounce all guardians and satanist parents who were assigned to me.	I announce that God is my heavenly Father and the Holy Spirit is my Guardian by whom I am sealed.
I renounce any baptism whereby I am identified with Satan.	I announce that I have been baptised into Christ Jesus and my identity is now in Him.
I renounce any sacrifice made on my behalf by which Satan may claim ownership of me.	I announce that only the sacrifice of Christ has any claim on me. I belong to Him. I have been purchased by the blood of the Lamb.

In addition to the lists above, all other satanic rituals, covenants, promises and assignments must be specifically renounced as the Lord brings them to your mind.

Step 2
Deception versus Truth

God's Word is true and we need to accept His truth in the innermost part of our being (see Psalm 51:6). Whether or not we *feel* it is true, we need to *believe* it is true! Jesus is the truth, the Holy Spirit is the Spirit of truth, the Word of God is truth and we are encouraged to speak the truth in love (see John 14:6; 16:13; 17:17; Ephesians 4:15).

The believer in Christ has no business deceiving others by lying, telling "white" lies, exaggerating, stretching the truth, or anything relating to falsehood. Satan is the father of lies, and he seeks to keep people in bondage through deception. It is the truth in Jesus that sets us free (see John 8:32–36,44; 2 Timothy 2:26; Revelation 12:9). We will find real joy and freedom when we stop living a lie and live openly in the truth. After confessing his sin, King David wrote, "How blessed [happy] is the man... in whose spirit there is no deceit!" (Psalm 32:2).

We have been called to walk in the light (see 1 John 1:7). When we are sure God loves and accepts us, we can be free to own up to our sins and face reality, instead of running and hiding from the truth and painful circumstances.

Start this Step by praying the following prayer aloud. Don't let any threatening, opposing thoughts, such as *This is a waste of time* or *I wish I could believe this but I just can't*, keep you from praying and choosing the truth. Even if this is difficult for you, work your way through this Step. God will strengthen you as you rely on Him.

Dear Heavenly Father,
I know that You want me to know the truth, believe the truth, speak the truth and live in accordance with the truth. Thank You that it is the truth that will set me free. In many ways I have been deceived by Satan, the father of lies, and I have deceived myself as well.

Father, I pray in the name of the Lord Jesus Christ, by virtue of His shed blood and resurrection, and ask You to rebuke all evil spirits that are deceiving me.

I have trusted in Jesus alone to save me, and so I am Your forgiven child in Christ. Therefore, since You accept me just as I am, I can be free to face my sin and not try to hide.

I ask for the Holy Spirit to guide me into all truth. I ask You to "search me, O God, and know my heart; try me and know my anxious thoughts; and see if there be any hurtful way in me, and lead me in the everlasting way." In the name of Jesus, who is the *Truth. Amen.*

(See Psalm 139:23,24.)

There are many ways in which Satan, "the god of this world", seeks to deceive us. Just as he did with Eve, the devil tries to convince us to rely on ourselves and to try to get our needs met through the world around us, rather than trusting in the provision of our Father in heaven.

The following exercise will help you discover ways you may have been deceived. Tick each area of deception that the Lord brings to your mind and confess it, using the prayer following the list.

Ways You Can be Deceived by the World

❏ Believing that acquiring money and things will bring me lasting happiness (see Matthew 13:22; 1 Timothy 6:10)

❏ Believing that excessive food and alcohol can relieve my stress and make me happy (see Proverbs 20:1; 23:19–21)

❏ Believing that an attractive body and personality will get me what I want (see Proverbs 31:10; 1 Peter 3:3,4)

❏ Believing that gratifying sexual lust will bring lasting satisfaction (see Ephesians 4:22; 1 Peter 2:11)

❏ Believing that I can sin and get away without any negative consequences (see Hebrews 3:12,13)

❏ Believing that I need more than what God has given me in Christ (see 2 Corinthians 11:2–4,13–15)

❏ Believing that I can do whatever I want and no one can touch me (see Proverbs 16:18; Obadiah 3; 1 Peter 5:5)

❏ Believing that people who refuse to accept Christ go to heaven anyway (see 1 Corinthians 6:9–11)

❏ Believing that I can associate with bad company and not become corrupted (see 1 Corinthians 15:33,34)

❏ Believing that I can read, see or listen to anything and not be corrupted (see Proverbs 4:23–27; 6:27,28; Matthew 5:28)

❏ Believing that there are no consequences on earth for my sins (see Galatians 6:7,8)

❏ Believing that I must gain the approval of certain people in order to be happy (see Galatians 1:10)

❏ Believing that I must measure up to certain standards in order to feel good about myself (see Galatians 3:2,3; 5:1)

Lord, I confess that I have been deceived by _____. I thank You for Your forgiveness, and I commit myself to believing only Your truth. In Jesus' name. Amen.

It is important to know that, in addition to being deceived by the world, false teachers and deceiving spirits, we can also deceive ourselves. Now that you are alive in Christ, completely forgiven and totally accepted, you don't need to defend yourself the way you used to. Christ is now your defence. Confess the ways the Lord shows you that you have deceived yourself or defended yourself wrongly, by using the following lists and prayers of confession:

Ways to Deceive Yourself

❑ Hearing God's Word but not doing what it says (see James 1:22)
❑ Saying I have no sin (see 1 John 1:8)
❑ Thinking I am something I'm really not (see Galatians 6:3)
❑ Thinking I am wise in this worldly age (see 1 Corinthians 3:18,19)
❑ Thinking I can be truly religious but not control my tongue (see James 1:26)

Lord, I confess that I have deceived myself by _____.
Thank You for Your forgiveness. I commit myself to believing only Your truth. In Jesus' name. Amen.

Ways to Defend Yourself Wrongly

❑ Denial of reality (conscious or unconscious)
❑ Fantasy (avoiding reality by daydreaming, TV, films, music, computer or video games, drugs, alcohol, etc.)
❑ Emotional insulation (withdrawing from people or keeping people at a distance to avoid rejection)
❑ Regression (reverting back to less threatening times)
❑ Displaced anger (taking out frustrations on innocent people)
❑ Projection (blaming others for my problems)

❏ Rationalisation (making excuses for my own poor behaviour)
❏ Lying (presenting a false image)

*Lord, I confess that I have defended myself wrongly through
_____. Thank You for Your forgiveness. I now com-
mit myself to trusting in You to defend and protect me. In
Jesus' name. Amen.*

Choosing the truth may be hard for you if you have believed lies for many years. You may need some ongoing help to weed out any defence mechanisms you have relied on to cope with life. Every Christian needs to learn that Christ is the only defence he or she needs. Realising that you are already forgiven and accepted by God through Christ will help to free you to place all your dependence on Him.

Faith is the biblical response to the truth, and believing what God says is simply a choice we can all make. If you say, "I wish I could believe God, but I just can't", you are being deceived. Of course you can believe God – because what God says is always true. Believing is something you *choose* to do, not something you *feel* like doing.

The Truth About Your Father God

Sometimes we are greatly hindered from walking by faith in our Father God because of lies we have believed about Him. The following exercise will help break the chains of those lies and enable you to begin to experience that intimate "Abba, Father" relationship with him.

Work your way down the list line by line, left to right. Begin each one with the statement in bold at the top of that list. Read through the lists *aloud*.

I renounce the lie that my Father God is...	I joyfully accept the truth that my Father God is...
distant and uninterested in me.	intimate and involved (see Psalm 139:1–18).
insensitive and uncaring.	kind and compassionate (see Psalm 103:8–14).
stern and demanding.	accepting and filled with joy and love (see Romans 15:7; Zephaniah 3:17).
passive and cold.	warm and affectionate (see Isaiah 40:11; Hosea 11:3,4).
absent or too busy for me.	always with me and eager to be with me (Hebrews 13:5; Jer. 31:20; Ezekiel 34:11–16).
impatient, angry or never satisfied with what I do.	patient and slow to anger and delights in those who put their hope in His unfailing love (Ex. 34:6; 2 Peter 3:9; Ps. 147:11).
mean, cruel or abusive.	is loving and gentle and protective (see Jeremiah 31:3; Isaiah 42:3; Psalm 18:2).
trying to take all the fun out of life.	trustworthy and wants to give me a full life; His will is good, perfect and acceptable for me (see Lamentations 3:22,23; John 10:10; Romans 12:1,2).
controlling or manipulative.	full of grace and mercy, and gives me freedom to fail (see Hebrews 4:15,16; Luke 15:11–16, 22–24).
condemning or unforgiving.	tender-hearted and forgiving; His heart and arms are always open to me (see Psalm 130:1–4; Luke 15:17–24).
nitpicking or a demanding perfectionist.	committed to my growth and proud of me as His growing child (Romans 8:28, 29; Hebrews 12:5–11; 2 Corinthians 7:14).

I am the apple of His eye!
(Deuteronomy 32:9–10, NIV)

If this is a difficult area for you, you will find it extremely helpful to say this declaration out loud every day for six weeks or so and to study the Bible passages in your quiet times.

ARE YOU FEARFUL AND ANXIOUS?

Anxiety and plaguing fears can control our lives and prevent us from walking by faith in the surpassing victory that is ours in Christ. If you feel that anxiety and fear are preventing you from living with boldness and confidence in God's presence and power in your life, you need to renounce them specifically to gain the freedom that is yours in Christ. (See Appendices A and B.)

The New Age movement has twisted the concept of faith by saying that we make something true by believing it. No, we can't create reality with our minds; only God creates reality. We can only *face* reality with our minds. Faith is choosing to believe and act upon what God says, regardless of feelings or circumstances. Believing something does not make it true. *It's true; therefore, we choose to believe it.*

Just "having faith" is not enough. The key question is whether what you believe in is real and trustworthy. If the object of your faith is not reliable, then no amount of believing will change it. That is why our faith must be on the solid rock of God and His Word. That is the only way to live a responsible and fruitful life. On the other hand, if what you believe in is not true, then you will not experience the freedom that only the truth can bring.

For generations, Christians have known the importance of publicly declaring what they believe. Read aloud the following statements of truth, thinking about what you are saying. You may find it very helpful to read it daily for several weeks to renew your mind with the truth and replace any lies you have believed.

Statements of Truth

1. *I recognise that there is only one true and living God, Who exists as the Father, Son and Holy Spirit. He is worthy of all honour, praise and glory as the One who made all things and holds all things together (see Exodus 20:2,3; Colossians 1:16,17).*

2. *I recognise that Jesus Christ is the Messiah, the Word who became flesh and dwelt among us. I believe that He came to destroy the works of the devil, and that He disarmed the rulers and authorities and made a public display of them, having triumphed over them by the cross (see John 1:1,14; Colossians 2:15; 1 John 3:8).*

3. *I believe that God demonstrated His own love for me in that while I was still a sinner, Christ died for me. I believe that He has delivered me from the dominion of darkness and transferred me to His kingdom, and in Him I have redemption, the forgiveness of sins (see Romans 5:8; Colossians 1:13,14).*

4. *I believe that I am now a child of God and that I am seated with Christ in the heavenly places. I believe that I was saved by the grace of God through faith, and that it was a gift and not a result of any works on my part (see Ephesians 2:6,8,9; 1 John 3:1–3).*

5. *I choose to be strong in the Lord and in the strength of His might. I put no confidence in the flesh, for the weapons of warfare are not of the flesh but are divinely powerful for the destruction of strongholds.*
   I put on the full armour of God. I resolve to stand firm in my faith and resist the evil one (see 2 Corinthians 10:4; Ephesians 6:10–20; Philippians 3:3).

6. *I believe that apart from Christ I can do nothing, so I declare my complete dependence on Him. I choose to remain in Christ in order to bear much fruit and glorify my Father. I announce to Satan that Jesus is my Lord. I reject any and all counterfeit gifts or works of Satan in my life (see John 15:5,8; 1 Corinthians 12:3).*

7. *I believe that the truth will set me free and that Jesus is the truth. If He sets me free, I will be free indeed. I recognise that walking in the light is the only path of true fellowship with God and man. Therefore, I stand against all of Satan's deceptions by taking every thought captive in obedience to Christ. I declare that the Bible is the only authoritative standard for truth and life (see John 8:32,36; 14:6; 2 Corinthians 10:5; 2 Timothy 3:15–17; 1 John 1:3–7).*

8. *I choose to present my body to God as a living and holy sacrifice and the parts of my body as instruments of righteousness. I choose to renew my mind by the living Word of God in order that I may prove that the will of God is good, acceptable and perfect. I put off the old self with its evil practices and put on the new self. I declare myself to be a new creation in Christ (see Romans 6:13; 12:1,2; 2 Corinthians 5:17; Colossians 3:9,10, NIV).*

9. *By faith, I choose to be filled with the Spirit so that I can be guided into all truth. I choose to walk by the Spirit so that I will not carry out the desires of the flesh (see John 16:13; Galatians 5:16; Ephesians 5:18).*

10. *I renounce all selfish goals and choose the ultimate goal of love. I choose to obey the two greatest commandments: to love the Lord my God with all my heart, soul, mind and strength and to love my neighbour as myself (see Matthew 22:37–39; 1 Timothy 1:5).*

11. *I believe that the Lord Jesus has all authority in heaven and on earth, and that He is the head over all rule and authority. I am complete in Him. I believe that Satan and his demons are subject to me in Christ since I am a member of Christ's body. Therefore, I obey the command to submit to God and resist the devil, and I command Satan in the name of Jesus Christ to leave my presence (see Matthew 28:18; Ephesians 1:19–23; Colossians 2:10; James 4:7).*

Step 3
Bitterness versus Forgiveness

We need to forgive others so that Satan cannot take advantage of us (see 2 Corinthians 2:10,11). We are commanded to get rid of all bitterness in our lives and forgive others as we have been forgiven (Ephesians 4:31,32). Ask God to bring to your mind the people you need to forgive by praying the following prayer aloud:

Dear Heavenly Father,
I thank You for the riches of Your kindness, forbearance and patience towards me, knowing that Your kindness has led me to repentance. I confess that I have not shown that same kindness and patience towards those who have hurt or offended me. Instead, I have held on to my anger, bitterness and resentment towards them. Please bring to my mind all the people I need to forgive in order that I may now do so. In Jesus' name. Amen.

(See Romans 2:4.)

On a separate sheet of paper, list the names of people who come to your mind. At this point don't question whether you need to forgive them or not. If a name comes to mind, write it down.

Often we hold things against ourselves as well, punishing ourselves for wrong choices we've made in the past. Write "Myself" at the bottom of your list if you need to forgive yourself. Forgiving yourself is simply accepting the truth that God has already forgiven you in Christ. If God forgives you, you can forgive yourself!

Also write down "Thoughts against God" at the bottom of your list. Obviously, God has never done anything wrong so we don't need to forgive Him. Sometimes, however, we harbour angry thoughts against Him because He did not do what we wanted Him to do. We must let them go (see Appendix D on page 82 for some prayers you can use to forgive yourself and forgive God).

Before you begin working through the process of forgiving those on your list, take a few minutes to review what forgiveness is and what it is not.

Forgiveness Is Not Forgetting

People who want to forget all that was done to them will find they cannot do it. Don't put off forgiving those who have hurt you, hoping the pain will one day go away. Once you choose to forgive someone, *then* Christ can come and begin to heal you of your hurts. But the healing cannot begin until you first forgive.

Forgiveness Is a Choice, a Decision of Your Will

Since God requires you to forgive, it is something you can do. Sometimes it is very hard to forgive someone because we naturally want revenge for the things we have suffered. Forgiveness seems to go against our sense of what is right and fair. So we hold on to our anger, trying to punish people over and over again in our minds for the pain they've caused us.

But we are told by God never to take our own revenge (see Romans 12:19). Let God deal with the person. Let him or her off your hook, because as long as you refuse to forgive someone, you are still hooked to that person. You are still chained to your past, bound up in your bitterness. By forgiving, you let the other person off your hook; but he or she is not off God's hook. You must trust that God will deal with the person justly and fairly, something you simply cannot do.

"But you don't know how much this person hurt me!" you say. You're right. We don't, but Jesus does, and He tells you to forgive others for your sake. Until you let go of your anger and hatred, the person is still hurting you. You can't turn back the clock and change the past, but you can be free from it. You can stop the pain, but there is only one way to do it – forgive from your heart.

Forgive others for your sake so you can be free from your past.

Forgiveness Is Agreeing to Live with the Consequences of Another Person's Sin

You are going to have to live with the consequences of what was done whether you like it or not. The only choice you have is whether you will do so in the *bondage of bitterness* or in the *freedom of forgiveness*. No one truly forgives without accepting and suffering the pain of another person's sin. That can seem unfair and you may wonder, "Where is the justice?". The cross makes forgiveness legally and morally right. Jesus died once for all our sins.

Jesus took the *eternal* consequences of sin upon Himself. God "made Him who knew no sin to be sin on our behalf, that we might become the righteousness of God in Him" (2 Corinthians 5:21). We, however, often suffer the temporary consequences of other people's sins. That is simply a harsh reality of life all of us have to face.

Do not wait for the other person to ask for your forgiveness. Remember, Jesus did not wait for those who were crucifying Him to apologise before He forgave them. Even while they mocked and jeered at him, He prayed, "Father, forgive them, for they do not know what they are doing" (Luke 23:34, NIV).

Forgiveness Comes From Your Heart

Allow God to bring the painful memories to the surface and then acknowledge how you feel towards those who've hurt you. If your forgiveness doesn't touch the emotional core of your life, it will be incomplete. Too often we're afraid of the pain so we bury our emotions deep down inside us. Let God bring them to the surface so He can begin to heal those damaged emotions.

Forgiveness Is Choosing Not to Hold Someone's Sin Against Him or Her Anymore

It is common for bitter people to bring up past issues with those who have hurt them. They want those who have hurt them to feel as bad as they do! But we must let go of the past and choose to reject any thought of revenge. This doesn't mean you continue to put up with the future sins of others. God does not tolerate sin and neither should you. Don't allow yourself to be continually abused by others. Take a stand against sin while continuing to exercise grace and forgiveness towards those who hurt you. If you need help setting scriptural boundaries to protect yourself from further abuse, talk to a trusted friend, counsellor or pastor.

Forgiveness Cannot Wait Until You Feel Like Forgiving

If you wait until you feel like forgiving, you will never get there. Make the hard choice to forgive even if you don't feel like it. Once you choose to forgive, Satan will lose his power over you in that area, and God will heal your damaged emotions. Freedom is what you will gain right now, not necessarily an immediate change in feelings.

Now you are ready to begin. Starting with the first person on your list, make the choice to forgive him or her for every painful memory that comes to your mind.

Continue until you are sure you have dealt with all the remembered pain caused by that individual. Then work your way down the list in the same way.

As you begin forgiving people, God may bring to your mind painful memories you've totally forgotten. Let Him do this even if it hurts. God wants you to be free; forgiving those people is the only way. Don't try to excuse the offender's behaviour, even if it is someone you are really close to.

Don't say, "Lord, please help me to forgive." He is already helping you and will be with you all the way through the process. Don't say, "Lord, I want to forgive" because that bypasses the hard choice we have to make. Say, "Lord, I *choose* to forgive..."

For every painful memory you have for each person on your list, pray aloud:

Lord,
I choose to forgive _____ *(name the person) for*
_____ *(what they did or failed to do), which*
made me feel _____ *(verbally tell the*
Lord every hurt and pain He brings to your mind).

After you have forgiven each person for all the offences that came to your mind, and after you have honestly expressed how you felt, conclude your forgiveness of that person by praying aloud:

Lord,
I choose not to hold on to my resentment. I thank You for
setting me free from the bondage of my bitterness. I let go of
my right to seek revenge and ask You to heal my damaged
emotions. I now ask You to bless _____ *(name the*
person). In Jesus' name. Amen.

Step 4

Rebellion versus Submission

We live in a rebellious age. Many people only obey laws and authorities when it is convenient for them. There is a general lack of respect for those in government, and Christians are often as guilty as the rest of society in fostering a critical, rebellious spirit. Certainly, we are not expected to agree with our leaders' policies that are in violation of the Bible, but we are to "honour all men [people]; love the brotherhood, fear God, honour the king" (1 Peter 2:17).

God established all governing authorities and requires us to be submissive (Romans 13:1–5; 1 Peter 2:13–17). Rebelling against God and the authorities He has set up is a very serious sin because it gives Satan an opportunity to attack. God requires more, however, than just the outward appearance of submission; He wants us to submit sincerely from the heart to those in authority. It is for your spiritual protection that you live under the authority of God and those He has placed over you.

The Bible makes it clear that we have two main responsibilities towards those in authority over us: to pray for them and to submit to them (see Romans 13:1–7; 1 Timothy 2:1,2). To commit yourself to that godly lifestyle, pray the following prayer aloud from your heart:

Dear Heavenly Father,
You have said in the Bible that rebellion is the same thing
as witchcraft and as bad as idolatry. I know I have not
always been submissive, but instead I have rebelled in my
heart against You and against those You have placed in
authority over me. I pray that You would show me all the
ways I have been rebellious. I choose now to adopt a sub-
missive spirit and a servant's heart. In Jesus' precious
name. Amen. (See 1 Samuel 15:23.)

Being under authority is clearly an act of faith! By submitting, you are trusting God to work through His established lines of authority, even when they are harsh or
unkind or tell you to do something you don't want to do.
There may be times when those over you abuse their
authority and break the laws that are ordained by God
for the protection of innocent people. In those cases, you
will need to seek help from a higher authority for your
protection. The law may require that such abuse be
reported to the police or other agency. If there is continuing abuse (physical, mental, emotional or sexual) where
you live, you may need further help to deal with that
situation.

If authorities abuse their position by requiring you to
break God's laws, or compromise your commitment to
Him, then you need to obey God rather than man (see
Acts 4:19,20). Be careful though. Don't assume that an
authority is violating God's Word just because they are
telling you to do something you don't like. We all need
to adopt a humble, submissive spirit to one another in
the fear of Christ (see Ephesians 5:21). In addition, however, God has set up specific lines of authority to protect
us and to give order to our daily lives.

As you prayerfully look over the next list, allow the
Lord to show you any specific ways in which you have

been rebellious to authority. Then, using the prayer of confession that follows the list, specifically confess whatever the Lord brings to your mind.

❑ Civil government including traffic laws, tax laws, attitude towards government officials (see Romans 13:1–7; 1 Timothy 2:1–4; 1 Peter 2:13–17)
❑ Parents, step-parents or legal guardians (see Ephesians 6:1–3)
❑ Teachers or other school officials (see Romans 13:1–4)
❑ Employers (past and present) (see 1 Peter 2:18–23)
❑ Husband (see 1 Peter 3:1–4) or wife (see Ephesians 5:21; 1 Peter 3:7) [*Note to husbands:* take a moment to ask the Lord if your lack of love for your wife could be fostering a rebellious spirit within her. If so, confess that now as a violation of Ephesians 5:22–33.]
❑ Church leaders (see Hebrews 13:7)
❑ God (see Daniel 9:5,9)

For each way in which the Spirit of God brings to your mind that you have been rebellious, use the following prayer to confess that sin specifically.

Lord, I confess that I have been rebellious towards _____ (name) by _____ (say what you did specifically). Thank You for forgiving my rebellion. I choose now to be submissive and obedient to Your Word. By the blood shed by the Lord Jesus Christ, I pray that all ground gained by evil spirits in my life due to my rebellion would be cancelled. In Jesus' name, I pray. Amen.

Step 5
Pride versus Humility

Pride kills. It says, "I don't need God's or anyone else's help. I can handle it by myself." Oh no, you can't! We absolutely need God, and we definitely need each other. The apostle Paul wisely wrote, "[We] worship in the Spirit of God and glory in Christ Jesus and *put no confidence in the flesh*" (Philippians 3:3, emphasis added). That is a good definition of humility: putting no confidence in the flesh, that is, in ourselves; but, rather, being *"strong in the Lord, and in the strength of His might"* (Ephesians 6:10, emphasis added). Humility is confidence properly placed in God.

Proverbs 3:5–7 expresses a similar thought: "Trust in the LORD with all your heart, and do not lean on your own understanding. In all your ways acknowledge Him, and He will make your paths straight. Do not be wise in your own eyes; fear the LORD and turn away from evil." (James 4:6–10 and 1 Peter 5:1–10 also warn us that serious spiritual problems will result when we are proud.) Use the prayer on the following page to express your commitment to living humbly before God:

Dear Heavenly Father,

You have said that pride goes before destruction and an arrogant spirit before stumbling. I confess that I have been thinking mainly of myself and not of others. I have not denied myself, picked up my cross daily, and followed You. As a result, I have given ground in my life to the devil. I have sinned by believing I could be happy and successful on my own. I confess that I have placed my will before Yours, and I have centred my life around myself instead of You.

I repent of my pride and selfishness and pray that all ground gained in me by the enemies of the Lord Jesus Christ would be cancelled. I choose to rely on the Holy Spirit's power and guidance, so I will do nothing from selfishness or conceit. With humility of mind, I will regard others as more important than myself. And I choose to make You, Lord, the centre of my life.

Please show me now all the specific ways in which I have lived my life in pride. Enable me through love to serve others and in honour to prefer others. I ask all of this in the gentle and humble name of Jesus, my Lord. Amen.

(See Proverbs 16:18; Matthew 6:33; 16:24;
Romans 12:10; Philippians 2:3.)

Having made that commitment to God in prayer, now allow Him to show you any specific ways in which you have lived in a proud manner. The following list may help you. As the Lord brings to your mind areas of pride, use the prayer on the next page to guide you in your confession.

- ❏ Having a stronger desire to do my will than God's

- ❏ Leaning too much on my own understanding and experience rather than seeking God's guidance

- ❏ Relying on my own strengths and abilities instead of depending on the power of the Holy Spirit

- ❏ Being more concerned about controlling others than developing self-control

- ❏ Being too busy doing "important" things to take time to do little things for others

- ❏ Having a tendency to think that I have no needs

- ❏ Finding it hard to admit when I am wrong

- ❏ Being more concerned about pleasing people than pleasing God

- ❏ Being concerned about getting the credit I feel I deserve

- ❏ Thinking I am more humble, spiritual, religious or devoted than others

- ❏ Being driven to obtain recognition by attaining degrees, titles or positions

- ❏ Often feeling that my needs are more important than another person's needs

- ❏ Considering myself better than others because of my abilities and accomplishments

- ❏ Other ways I have thought more highly of myself than I should _____

For each of the above areas that has been true in your life, pray aloud:

Lord,
I agree I have been proud in _____(name the
area). Thank You for forgiving me for my pride. I choose to
humble myself before You and others. I choose to place all
my confidence in You and none in my flesh. In Jesus' name.
Amen.

Dealing with Prejudice and Bigotry

Pride is the original sin of the devil. It sets one person or group against another. Satan's strategy is always to divide and conquer, but God has given us a ministry of reconciliation (2 Corinthians 5:19). Consider for a moment the work of Christ in breaking down the long-standing barrier of racial prejudice between Jew and Gentile:

> For [Christ] is our peace, who has made the two one and has destroyed the barrier, the dividing wall of hostility, by abolishing in His flesh the law with its commandments and regulations. His purpose was to create in Himself one new man out of the two, thus making peace, and in this one body to reconcile both of them to God through the cross, by which He put to death their hostility. He came and preached peace to you who were far away and peace to those who were near. For through Him we both have access to the Father by one Spirit (Ephesians 2:14–18, NIV).

Many times we deny that there is prejudice or bigotry in our hearts, yet "nothing in all creation is hidden from God's sight. Everything is uncovered and laid bare before the eyes of Him to whom we must give account"

(Hebrews 4:13, NIV). The following is a prayer asking God to shine His light upon your heart and reveal any area of proud prejudice:

Dear Heavenly Father, I know that You love all people equally and that You do not show favouritism. You accept people from every nation who fear You and do what is right. You do not judge them based on skin colour, race, economic standing, ethnic background, gender, denominational preference or any other worldly matter. I confess that I have too often prejudged others or regarded myself as superior. I have not always been a minister of reconciliation but have been a proud agent of division through my attitudes, words and deeds. I repent of all hateful bigotry and proud prejudice, and I ask You, Lord, now to reveal to my mind all the specific ways in which this form of pride has corrupted my heart and mind. In Jesus' name. Amen.

(See Acts 10:34; 2 Corinthians 5:16.)

For each area of prejudice, superiority or bigotry that the Lord brings to mind, pray the following prayer aloud from your heart:

I confess and renounce the sin of prejudice against _____(name the group). I thank You for Your forgiveness, Lord, and ask now that You would change my heart and make me a loving agent of reconciliation with _____(name the group). In Jesus' name. Amen.

Step 6

Bondage versus Freedom

Many times we feel trapped in a vicious cycle of sin-confess-sin-confess that never seems to end. We can become very discouraged and end up just giving up and giving in to the sins of our flesh. To find freedom we must follow James 4:7: "Submit therefore to God. Resist the devil and he will flee from you." We submit to God by confessing our sin and repenting (turning away from sin). We resist the devil by rejecting his lies. Instead, put on the full armour of God and walk in the truth (see Ephesians 6:10–20).

Sin that has become a habit often requires us to ask a trusted brother or sister in Christ to hold us accountable. James 5:16 says, "Therefore, confess your sins to one another, and pray for one another, so that you may be healed. The effective prayer of a righteous man can accomplish much." Sometimes the assurance of 1 John 1:9 is enough: "If we confess our sins, He is faithful and righteous to forgive us our sins and to cleanse us from all unrighteousness."

Remember, confession is not saying, "I'm sorry"; it is openly admitting, "I did it". Whether you need help from other people or just the accountability of walking in the light before God, pray the following prayer aloud:

Dear Heavenly Father,
You have told me to put on the Lord Jesus Christ and to make no provision for the flesh. I confess that I have given in to fleshly passions that wage war against my soul. I thank You that in Christ my sins are already forgiven, but I have broken Your holy law and given the devil a chance to wage war in my body. I come to You now to confess and renounce these sins of the flesh so that I might be cleansed and set free from the bondage of sin. Please reveal to my mind all the sins of the flesh I have committed and the ways I have grieved the Holy Spirit. In Jesus' holy name. Amen.

(See Proverbs 28:13, NIV; Romans 6:12-13; 13:14; 2 Corinthians 4:2; James 4:1; 1 Peter 2:11; 5:8.)

The following list contains many sins of the flesh, but a prayerful examination of Mark 7:20–23, Galatians 5:19–21, Ephesians 4:25–31 and other Bible passages will help you to be even more thorough. Look over the list below and the passages just mentioned and ask the Holy Spirit to bring to your mind the ones you need to confess. He may reveal to you others as well. For each one the Lord shows you, pray a prayer of confession from your heart. There is a sample prayer following the list.

(Note: Sexual sins, divorce, eating disorders, substance abuse, abortion, suicidal tendencies, and perfectionism will be dealt with later in this Step. Further help may be necessary to find complete healing and freedom in these and other areas. Ask a pastor or other trusted Christian leader for advice.)

- ❏ Stealing
- ❏ Quarrelling/fighting
- ❏ Jealousy/envy
- ❏ Complaining/criticising
- ❏ Being judgmental
- ❏ Sarcasm
- ❏ Gossip/slander
- ❏ Swearing
- ❏ Competitiveness
- ❏ Apathy/laziness
- ❏ Lying
- ❏ Hatred
- ❏ Anger
- ❏ Lustful thoughts and actions
- ❏ Drunkenness
- ❏ Cheating
- ❏ Procrastination (putting things off)
- ❏ Greed/materialism
- ❏ Others:

Lord,
I confess that I have committed the sin of _____
(name the sin). Thank You for Your forgiveness and cleansing. I now turn away from this sin and turn to You, Lord. Strengthen me by Your Holy Spirit to obey You. In Jesus' name. Amen.

It is our responsibility not to allow sin to have control over our bodies. We must not use our bodies or another person's body as an instrument of unrighteousness (see Romans 6:12–13). Sexual immorality is not only a sin against God, but is sin against your body, the temple of the Holy Spirit (see 1 Corinthians 6:18,19). To find freedom from sexual sin, begin by praying the following prayer:

Lord,
I ask You to bring to my mind every sexual use of my body as an instrument of unrighteousness so that, in Christ, I can renounce these sexual sins and break their bondages. In Jesus' name. Amen.

As the Lord brings to your mind every wrong sexual use of your body, whether it was done to you (rape, incest, sexual molestation) or willingly by you (pornography, masturbation, sexual immorality), renounce every occasion:

Lord,
I renounce _____*(name the specific use of*
your body) with _____*(name any other*
person involved). I ask You to break that sinful bond with
_____*(name).*

After you have finished, commit your body to the Lord by praying:

Lord,
I renounce all these uses of my body as an instrument of
unrighteousness, and I admit to any wilful
participation. I choose now to present my eyes, mouth,
mind, heart, hands, feet and sexual organs to You as instru-
ments of righteousness. I present my whole body to You as a
living sacrifice, holy and acceptable. I choose to reserve the
sexual use of my body only for marriage.

I reject the devil's lie that my body is not clean or that it
is dirty or in any way unacceptable to You as a result of my
past sexual experiences. Lord, thank You that You have
totally cleansed and forgiven me and that You love and
accept me just the way I am. Therefore, I choose now to
accept myself and my body as clean in Your eyes. In Jesus'
name. Amen.

(See Hebrews 13:4.)

Special Prayers For Special Needs

Divorce

Lord,
I confess to You any part that I played in my divorce (ask the
Lord to show you specifics). Thank You for Your forgiveness,
and I choose not to condemn myself. I renounce the lie that
divorce affects my identity in Christ. I am a child of God,
and I reject the lie that I am a second-class Christian
because of the divorce. I reject the lie that says I am worth-
less, unlovable, and that my life is empty and meaningless.
I am complete in Christ who loves me and accepts me just
as I am. Lord, I commit the healing of all hurts in my life to
You as I have chosen to forgive those who have hurt me. I
also place my future in Your hands and choose to seek
human companionship in Your church. I surrender to Your
will as to whether or not I should get married again. I pray
all this in the healing name of Jesus, my Saviour, Lord, and
closest friend. Amen.

Homosexuality

Lord,
I renounce the lie that You have created me or anyone else
to be homosexual and I agree that in Your Word You clearly
forbid homosexual behaviour. I choose to accept myself as a
child of God and I thank You that You created me as a man
(woman). I renounce all homosexual thoughts, urges, drives
and acts and renounce all ways that Satan has used these
things to pervert my relationships. I announce that I am
free in Christ to relate to the opposite sex and my own sex
in the way that You intended. In Jesus' name. Amen.

Abortion

Lord,
I confess that I was not a proper guardian and keeper of the life You entrusted to me, and I admit that as sin. Thank You that because of Your forgiveness, I can forgive myself. I recognise that the child is in Your caring hands for all eternity. In Jesus' name. Amen.

Suicidal Tendencies

Lord,
I renounce all suicidal thoughts and any attempts I've made to take my own life or in any way injure myself. I renounce the lie that life is hopeless and that I can find peace and freedom by taking my own life. Satan is a thief and comes to steal, kill and destroy. I choose life in Christ who said He came to give me life and give it abundantly. Thank You for Your forgiveness that allows me to forgive myself. I choose to believe the truth that there is always hope in Christ. In Jesus' name. Amen.

(See John 10:10.)

Substance Abuse

Lord,
I confess that I have misused substances (alcohol, tobacco, food, prescription or street drugs) for the purpose of pleasure, to escape reality, or to cope with difficult problems. I confess that I have abused my body and programmed my mind in a harmful way. I have quenched the Holy Spirit as well. Thank You for forgiving me. I renounce any satanic connection or influence in my life through my misuse of food or chemicals. I cast my anxieties onto Christ who loves me. I commit myself to yield no longer to substance abuse, but instead I choose to allow the Holy Spirit to direct and empower me. In Jesus' name. Amen.

Eating Disorders or Self-Mutilation

Lord,

I renounce the lie that my value as a person is dependent upon my appearance or performance. I renounce cutting or abusing myself, vomiting, using laxatives or starving myself as a means of being in control, altering my appearance or trying to cleanse myself of evil. I announce that only the blood of the Lord Jesus cleanses me from sin. I realise I have been bought with a price and my body, the temple of the Holy Spirit, belongs to God. Therefore, I choose to glorify God in my body. I renounce the lie that I am evil or that any part of my body is evil. Thank You that You accept me just the way I am in Christ. In Jesus' name, I pray. Amen.

Drivenness and Perfectionism

Lord,

I renounce the lie that my self-worth depends on my ability to perform. I announce the truth that my identity and sense of worth are found in who I am as Your child. I renounce seeking the approval and acceptance of other people, and I choose to believe that I am already approved and accepted in Christ because of His death and resurrection for me. I choose to believe the truth that I have been saved, not by deeds done in righteousness, but according to Your mercy. I choose to believe that I am no longer under the curse of the law because Christ became a curse for me. I receive the free gift of life in Christ and choose to abide in Him. I renounce striving for perfection by living under the law. By Your grace, Heavenly Father, I choose from this day forward to walk by faith in the power of Your Holy Spirit according to what You have said is true. In Jesus' name. Amen.

After you have confessed all known sin, end this Step by praying:

Dear Heavenly Father,
I now confess these sins to You and claim forgiveness and cleansing through the blood of the Lord Jesus Christ. I cancel all ground that evil spirits have gained through my wilful involvement in sin. I ask this in the wonderful name of my Lord and Saviour, Jesus Christ. Amen.

Step 7

Curses versus Blessings

The next Step to freedom is to renounce the sins of your ancestors as well as any satanic assignments directed towards you or your ministry. In the Ten Commandments, God said:

> You shall not make for yourself an idol, or any likeness of what is in heaven above or on the earth beneath or in the water under the earth. You shall not worship them or serve them; for I, the LORD your God, am a jealous God, visiting the iniquity of the fathers on the children, on the third and the fourth generations of those who hate Me, but showing lovingkindness to thousands, to those who love Me and keep My commandments (Exodus 20:4–6).

The iniquities of one generation can adversely affect future generations unless the sins of ancestors are confessed and renounced, and your spiritual heritage in Christ is claimed. You are not guilty for the sin of your ancestors, but because of their sin, you may be predisposed to certain strengths or weaknesses and be influenced by the physical and spiritual atmosphere in which you were raised. These conditions can contribute towards causing someone to struggle with a particular sin. Ask the Lord to show you specifically what sins are characteristic of your family by praying the following prayer:

Dear Heavenly Father, I ask You to reveal to my mind now all the sins of my ancestors that are being passed down through family lines. I want to be free from those influences and walk in my new identity as a child of God. In Jesus' name. Amen.

As the Lord brings those areas of family sin to your mind, list them below.

1.

2.

3.

4.

5.

6.

7.

8.

9.

10.

Declaration

I here and now reject and disown all the sins of my ancestors. I specifically renounce the sins of _____ (name the areas of family sin the Lord revealed to you).

As one who has been delivered from the dominion of darkness into the kingdom of God's Son, I announce that the sins and iniquities of my ancestors have no hold on me and I now stand forgiven and cleansed in Christ.

As one who has been crucified and raised with Jesus Christ and who sits with Him in heavenly places, I renounce all curses that are directed towards me and my ministry. I announce the truth that Jesus has broken every curse that Satan and his workers have put on me.

I announce to Satan and all his forces that Christ became a curse for me when He died for my sins on the Cross. I reject any and every way in which Satan may claim ownership of me. I belong to the Lord Jesus Christ who purchased me with His own blood. I reject all blood sacrifices whereby Satan may claim ownership of me. I declare myself to be fully and eternally signed over and committed to the Lord Jesus Christ.

By the authority I have in Christ, I now command every enemy of the Lord Jesus to leave my presence.

I commit myself to my Heavenly Father to do His will from this day forward. In Jesus' name. Amen.

(See Galatians 3:13.)

Concluding Prayer

Dear Heavenly Father, I come to You as Your child, bought out of slavery to sin by the blood of the Lord Jesus Christ. You are the Lord of the universe and the Lord of my life. I submit my body to You as an instrument of righteousness, a living and holy sacrifice that will glorify You. I now ask You to fill me to overflowing with Your Holy Spirit today and every day. I commit myself to the renewing of my mind in order to prove that Your will is good, pleasing and perfect for me. All this I pray in the name and authority of the risen Lord Jesus Christ. Amen.

SEEKING THE FORGIVENESS OF OTHERS

Now that you have found your freedom in Christ, there may be an additional step for you to take. In Step Three you dealt with the need to forgive others who have offended you – a resolution between you and God. You may need to seek the forgiveness of those you have offended. You need to know if and when to take that further step and how to do it in a wise and Godly manner. (See Appendix C.)

Maintaining Your Freedom

Even after finding freedom in Christ by going through these seven Steps, you may come under attack hours, days, or even weeks later. But you don't have to give in to the world, the flesh or the devil. As you continue to walk in humble submission to God, you can resist the devil and he *will* flee from you (see James 4:7).

The devil is attracted to sin like flies are attracted to rotting rubbish. Get rid of the rubbish and the flies will depart for smellier places. In the same way, walk in the truth, confessing all sin and forgiving those who hurt you, and the devil will have no place in your life.

Realise that one victory does not mean the battles are over. *Freedom must be maintained.* After completing these Steps to Freedom, one happy lady asked, "Will I always be like this?" The answer is, she will maintain her freedom as long as she remains in a right relationship with God. But even if she slips and falls, she will know how to get right with God again.

One victim of horrible atrocities shared this illustration:

It was like being forced to play a game with an ugly stranger in my own home. I kept losing and wanting to quit but the ugly stranger wouldn't let me. Finally, I called the police (a higher authority), and they came and escorted the stranger out. He knocked on the door trying to regain entry, but this time I recognised his voice and didn't let him in.

What a beautiful picture of gaining and keeping your freedom in Christ! We call upon Jesus, the ultimate authority, and He escorts the enemy of our souls away from us.

How to Maintain Your Freedom

You must maintain your freedom. We cannot emphasise that enough. You have won a very important battle in an ongoing war. Freedom will continue to be yours as long as you keep choosing the truth and standing firm in the strength of the Lord. If you become aware of lies you have believed, renounce them and choose the truth. If new, painful memories surface, forgive those who hurt you. If the Lord shows you other areas of sin in your life, confess those promptly. This book can serve as a constant guide for you in dealing with the things God points out to you. Some people have found it helpful to walk through the Steps to Freedom in Christ again on a regular basis as a kind of spiritual check-up. As you do, read the instructions carefully.

For your encouragement and growth, we recommend that you read *The Bondage Breaker* (adult or youth versions), *Victory Over the Darkness* (or the youth version, *Stomping Out the Darkness*), *Walking in Freedom* (a 21-day follow-up devotional), and *Living Free*. To maintain your freedom in Christ, we strongly suggest the following as well.

1. Be involved in a loving, caring church fellowship where you can be open and honest with others and where God's truth is taught with grace.
2. Read and meditate on the Bible daily. Memorise key verses from the Steps to Freedom in Christ. You may

want to read the Statements of Truth (see Step 2) aloud daily and study the verses mentioned.

3. Learn to take every thought captive to the obedience of Christ. Assume responsibility for your thought life. Don't let your mind become passive. Reject all lies, choose to focus on the truth, and stand firm in your true identity as a child of God in Christ.

4. Don't drift back to old patterns of thinking, feeling and acting. This can happen very easily if you become spiritually and mentally lazy. If you are struggling with walking in the truth, share your battles openly with a trusted friend who will pray for you and encourage you to stand firm.

5. Don't expect other people to fight your battles for you, however. They can help you, but they can't think, pray, read the Bible or choose the truth for you.

6. Commit yourself to daily prayer. Prayer demonstrates a life of trusting in and depending on God. You can pray the following prayers often and with confidence. Let the words come from your heart as well as your lips and feel free to change them to make them *your* prayers.

Daily Prayer and Declaration

Dear Heavenly Father,
I praise You and honour You as my Lord and Saviour. You are in control of all things. I thank You that You are always with me and will never leave me nor forsake me. You are the only all-powerful and only wise God. You are kind and loving in all Your ways. I love You and thank You that I am united with Christ and spiritually alive in Him. I choose not to love the world or the things in the world, and I crucify the flesh and all its passions.

Thank You for the life I now have in Christ. I ask You to fill me with the Holy Spirit so I may say no to sin and yes to You. I declare my total dependence upon You and

I take my stand against Satan and all his lying ways. I choose to believe the truth of God's Word despite what my feelings may say. I refuse to be discouraged; You are the God of all hope. Nothing is too difficult for You. I am confident that You will supply all my needs as I seek to live according to Your Word. I thank You that I can be content and live a responsible life through Christ who strengthens me.

I now take my stand against Satan and command him and all his evil spirits to depart from me. I choose to put on the full armour of God so I may be able to stand firm against all the devil's schemes. I submit my body as a living and holy sacrifice to God, and I choose to renew my mind by the living Word of God. By so doing I will be able to prove that the will of God is good, pleasing and perfect for me. In the name of my Lord and Saviour, Jesus Christ. Amen.

Bedtime Prayer

Thank You, Lord, that You have brought me into Your family and have blessed me with every spiritual blessing in the heavenly places in Christ Jesus. Thank You for this time of renewal and refreshment through sleep. I accept it as one of Your blessings for Your children and I trust You to guard my mind and my body during my sleep.

As I have thought about You and Your truth during the day, I choose to let those good thoughts continue in my mind while I am asleep. I commit myself to You for Your protection against every attempt of Satan and his demons to attack me during sleep. Guard my mind from nightmares. I renounce all fear and cast every anxiety upon You, Lord. I commit myself to You as my rock, my fortress and my strong tower. May Your peace be upon this place of rest now. In the strong name of the Lord Jesus Christ. Amen.

Prayer for Cleansing Your Home

After removing and destroying all objects of false worship, pray this prayer aloud in every room if necessary:

Heavenly Father,
I acknowledge that You are the Lord of heaven and earth.
In Your sovereign power and love, You have given me all
things to enjoy. Thank You for this place to live. I claim
my home as a place of spiritual safety for me and my
family and ask for Your protection from all the attacks of
the enemy. As a child of God, raised up and seated with
Christ in the heavenly places, I command every evil spirit
claiming ground in this place, based on the activities of
past or present occupants, including me, to leave and
never return. I renounce all curses and spells directed
against this place. I ask You, Heavenly Father, to post
Your holy, warring angels around this place to guard it
from any and all attempts of the enemy to enter and dis-
turb Your purposes for me and my family. I thank You,
Lord, for doing this in the name of the Lord Jesus Christ.
Amen.

Prayer for Living in a Non-Christian Environment

After removing and destroying all objects of false worship in your possession, pray this aloud in the place where you live:

Thank You, Heavenly Father, for a place to live and to be
renewed by sleep. I ask You to set aside my room (or por-
tion of this room) as a place of spiritual safety for me. I
renounce any allegiance given to false gods or spirits by
other occupants. I renounce any claim to this room

(space) by Satan based on the activities of past or present occupants, including me. On the basis of my position as a child of God and joint-heir with Christ, who has all authority in heaven and on earth, I command all evil spirits to leave this place and never return. I ask You, Heavenly Father, to station Your holy, warring angels to protect me while I live here. In Jesus' mighty name. Amen.

Continue to walk in the truth that your identity and sense of worth come through who you are in Christ. Renew your mind with the truth that your acceptance, security and significance are in Christ alone.

We recommend that you meditate daily on the truths on the following pages. Try reading the entire list aloud, morning and evening, for the next few weeks. Think about what you are reading and let your heart rejoice in the truth.

In Christ I am accepted

I renounce the lie that I am rejected, unloved, dirty or shameful, because in Christ I am completely accepted. God says that:

I am God's child (see John 1:12)
I am Christ's friend (see John 15:15)
I have been justified (see Romans 5:1)
I am united with the Lord and I am one spirit with Him (see 1 Corinthians 6:17)
I have been bought with a price: I belong to God (see 1 Corinthians 6:19–20)
I am a member of Christ's body (see 1 Corinthians 12:27)
I am a saint, a holy one (see Ephesians 1:1)
I have been adopted as God's child (see Ephesians 1:5)
I have direct access to God through the Holy Spirit (see Ephesians 2:18)
I have been redeemed and forgiven of all my sins (see Colossians 1:14)
I am complete in Christ (see Colossians 2:10)

In Christ I am secure

I renounce the lie that I am guilty, unprotected, alone, or abandoned, because in Christ I am totally secure. God says that:

I am free forever from condemnation (see Romans 8:1,2)

I am assured that all things work together for good (see Romans 8:28)

I am free from any condemning charges against me (see Romans 8:31–34)

I cannot be separated from the love of God (see Romans 8:35–39)

I have been established, anointed, and sealed by God (see 2 Corinthians 1:21–22)

I am confident that the good work God has begun in me will be perfected (see Philippians 1:6)

I am a citizen of heaven (see Philippians 3:20)

I am hidden with Christ in God (see Colossians 3:3)

I have not been given a spirit of fear, but of power, love and a sound mind (see 2 Timothy 1:7)

I can find grace and mercy to help in time of need (see Hebrews 4:16)

I am born of God and the evil one cannot touch me (see 1 John 5:18)

In Christ I am significant

I renounce the lie that I am worthless, inadequate, helpless or hopeless, because in Christ I am deeply significant. God says that:

I am the salt of the earth and the light of the world (see Matthew 5:13,14)

I am a branch of the true vine, Jesus, a channel of his life (see John 15:1,5)

I have been chosen and appointed by God to bear fruit (see John 15:16)

I am a personal, Spirit-empowered witness of Christ (see Acts 1:8)

I am a temple of God (see 1 Corinthians 3:16)

I am a minister of reconciliation for God (see 2 Corinthians 5:17–21)

I am God's fellow worker (see 2 Corinthians 6:1)

I am seated with Christ in the heavenly realms (see Ephesians 2:6)

I am God's workmanship, created for good works (see Ephesians 2:10)

I may approach God with freedom and confidence (see Ephesians 3:12)

I can do all things through Christ who strengthens me! (see Philippians 4:13)

I am not the great "I Am", but by the grace of God I am what I am.

(See Exodus 3:14; John 8:24,28,58; 1 Corinthians 15:10.)

Appendix A – Resolving Anxiety

Anxiety is different from fear in that it lacks an object or adequate cause. People are anxious because they are uncertain about a specific outcome or don't know what is going to happen tomorrow. It is normal to be concerned about things we value; not to do so would demonstrate a lack of care.

One can be temporarily anxious about a forthcoming examination, attendance at a planned function, or the threat of an impending storm. Such concerns are normal and should ordinarily move one to responsible action. For some, the anxiety is more intense and prolonged. They struggle with a large number of worries and spend a lot of time and energy doing so. The intensity and frequency of the worrying are always out of proportion to the actual problem.

If persistent anxiety is a problem in your life, this Anxiety Worksheet can help you to cast all your anxieties on Christ because He cares for you (see 1 Peter 5:7).

Pray

Prayer is the first step in casting all your anxiety on Christ. Remember Paul's word, "Be anxious for nothing, but in everything by prayer and supplication with thanksgiving let your requests be made known to God" (Philippians 4:6). Ask God to guide you by expressing the following prayer:

Dear Heavenly Father,
I come to You as Your child purchased by the blood of the
Lord Jesus Christ. I declare my dependence upon You,
and I acknowledge my need of You. I know that apart
from Christ I can do nothing. You know the thoughts and
intentions of my heart and You know the situation I am
in from the beginning to the end. I feel as though I am
double-minded, and I need Your peace to guard my heart
and my mind. I humble myself before You and choose to
trust You to exalt me at the proper time in any way You
choose. I place my trust in You to supply all my needs
according to Your riches in glory and to guide me into all
truth. I ask for Your divine guidance so that I may fulfil
my calling to live a responsible life by faith in the power
of Your Holy Spirit. "Search me, O God, and know my
heart; try me and know my anxious thoughts; and see if
there be any hurtful way in me, and lead me in the ever-
lasting way" (Psalm 139: 23,24). In Jesus' precious
name. Amen.

Resolve Any Personal and Spiritual Conflicts

The purpose of the Steps to Freedom in Christ is to help
you get radically right with God and eliminate any possible influences of the devil on your mind. Remember,
"The Spirit clearly says that in later times some will aban-
don the faith and follow deceiving spirits and things
taught by demons" (1 Timothy 4:1, NIV). You will be a
double-minded person if you pay attention to a deceiving spirit. You need to have the presence of God in order
to have "the peace of God, which transcends all understanding, [that] will guard your hearts and your minds in
Christ Jesus" (Philippians 4:7, NIV).

State the Problem

A problem well-stated is half-solved. In anxious states of mind, people typically can't see the wood for the trees. Put the problem in perspective: will it matter for eternity? Generally speaking, the process of worrying takes a greater toll on a person than the negative consequences of what they worried about. Many anxious people find tremendous relief by simply having their problem clarified and put into perspective.

Divide the Facts from the Assumptions

People may be fearful of the facts, but not anxious. Fear has an object, and we'll be dealing with that in the following exercise. We're anxious because we don't know what is going to happen tomorrow. Since we don't know, we make assumptions. A peculiar trait of the mind is its tendency to assume the worst. If the assumption is accepted as truth, it will drive the mind to its anxiety limits. If you make presumptions about tomorrow, you will suffer the negative consequences, or stress and anxiety. "Anxiety in the heart of a man weighs it down" (Proverbs 12:25). Therefore, as best as possible, verify all assumptions.

Determine What You Have the Right or Ability to Control

You are responsible only for that which you have the right and ability to control. You are not responsible for that which you don't. Your sense of worth is tied only to that for which you are responsible. If you aren't living a responsible life, you should feel anxious! Don't try to cast your responsibility onto Christ – He will throw it back to you. But do cast your anxiety onto Him, because His integrity is at stake in meeting your needs if you are living a responsible and righteous life.

List What Is Your Responsibility

You need to commit yourself to be a responsible person and fulfil your calling and obligations in life.

The Rest Is God's Responsibility

Your only remaining responsibility is to continue to pray and focus on the truth according to Philippians 4:6–8. Any residual anxiety is probably due to your assuming responsibilities that God never intended you to have.

Anxiety Worksheet

Go to God in prayer.

Resolve all known personal and spiritual conflicts.

State the problem.

Divide the facts from assumptions.

- Facts relating to the situation:

- Assumptions relating to the situation:

Which assumptions can be verified as facts?

Determine what you have the right or ability to control.

- What you can control as a matter of personal responsibility:

- What you have no right or ability to control:

List everything related to the situation that is your responsibility.

If you have fulfilled your responsibility, the rest is God's responsibility, except for your continuing walk with God in prayer according to Philippians 4:6–8.

Appendix B – Steps to Overcoming Fear

If you have successfully resolved your personal and spiritual conflicts by submitting to God and resisting the devil, then you are ready to analyse your fears and work out a responsible course of action.

Analyse Your Fear Under God's Authority and Guidance

Begin by praying the following prayer aloud:

Dear Heavenly Father,
I come to You as Your child. I put myself under Your protective care and acknowledge that You are the only legitimate fear object in my life. I confess that I have been fearful and anxious because of my lack of trust and unbelief. I have not always lived by faith in You and too often I have relied on my own strength and resources. I thank You that I am forgiven in Christ.

I choose to believe the truth that You have not given me a spirit of fear, but of power, love and a sound mind (2 Timothy 1:7). Therefore I renounce any spirit of fear. I ask You to reveal to my mind all the fears that have been controlling me. Show me how I have become fearful and the lies I have believed. I desire to live a responsible life in the power of Your Holy Spirit. Show me how these fears have kept me from doing that. I ask this so that I can confess, renounce and overcome every fear by faith in You. In Jesus' name. Amen.

The following list may help you recognise some of the fears that have been hindering your walk of faith. On a separate sheet, write down the ones that apply to you, as well as any others not on the list which the Spirit of God has revealed to you. As you prayerfully recall your past, write a brief description of what happened and when, in order to trigger that fear.

- ❑ Fear of Satan
- ❑ Fear of divorce
- ❑ Fear of death
- ❑ Fear of not being loved by God
- ❑ Fear of never being loved
- ❑ Fear of not being able to love others
- ❑ Fear of marriage
- ❑ Fear of rejection by people
- ❑ Fear of never getting married
- ❑ Fear of never having children
- ❑ Fear of disapproval
- ❑ Fear of embarrassment
- ❑ Fear of failure
- ❑ Fear of being/becoming homosexual

- ❑ Fear of financial problems
- ❑ Fear of going crazy
- ❑ Fear of being a hopeless case
- ❑ Fear of the death of a loved one
- ❑ Fear of the future
- ❑ Fear of confrontation
- ❑ Fear of being victimised by crime
- ❑ Fear of having committed the unpardonable sin
- ❑ Fear of specific people, animals or objects
- ❑ Other specific fears the Lord brings to mind

  _____
  _____
  _____

The root of any unreasonable fear is a belief that is not based in truth. These false beliefs need to be rooted out and replaced by the truth of God's Word. Take as much time in prayer as you need to discern these lies, because renouncing them and choosing the truth is a critical step towards gaining and maintaining your freedom in Christ. You have to know and choose to believe the truth in order for it to set you free. Write down the lies you have believed for every fear, and the corresponding truth from the Word of God.

Ways You Have Been Living Under the Control of Fear

The next step is to determine how fear has prevented you from living a responsible life, compelled you to be irresponsible, or compromised your Christian witness. After you have gained the necessary insights into your fear, it is time to experience God's cleansing through confession and repentance (see 1 John 1:9; Proverbs 28:13). Confession is agreeing with God that what you did was sinful. Repentance is the choice to turn away from sin and walk by faith in God. Express the following prayer for each of the fears that you have analysed above:

Dear Lord,
I confess and repent of the fear of _____. I have believed (state the lie). I renounce that lie and I choose to believe the truth (state the truth). I also confess any and all ways this fear has resulted in living irresponsibly, or in compromising my witness for Christ (be specific).

I now choose to live by faith in You, Lord, believing Your promise that You will protect me and meet all my needs (Psalm 27:1; Matthew 6:33,34).

In Jesus' trustworthy name. Amen.

After working through every fear the Lord has revealed to you (including their accompanying lies and sinful behaviour), pray the following prayer:

Dear Heavenly Father,
I thank You that You are indeed trustworthy. I choose to believe You, even when my feelings and circumstances tell me to fear. You have told me not to fear, for You are with me; not to look about me anxiously for You are my God. You will strengthen me, help me, and surely uphold me with Your righteous right hand. In Jesus' mighty name. Amen. (See Isaiah 41:10.)

Work Out a Plan of Responsible Behaviour

The next step is to face the fear and prayerfully work out a plan to overcome it. Somebody once said, "Do the thing you fear the most and the death of fear is certain." Fear is like a mirage in the desert. It seems so real until you move towards it, but then it disappears into thin air. As long as we back away from fear, it will haunt us and grow in size, becoming like a giant.

Determine in Advance What Your Response Will be to any Fear Object

The fear of God is the one fear that can dispel all other fears, because God rules supreme over every other fear object, including Satan. Even though, "your adversary, the devil, prowls about like a roaring lion, seeking someone to devour" (1 Peter 5:8), he has been defeated. "Having disarmed the powers and authorities, [Jesus] made a public spectacle of them, triumphing over them by the cross" (Colossians 2:15, NIV).

The presence of any fear object should prompt us to focus on God who is always present and all powerful. To worship God is to acknowledge and ascribe to Him His divine attributes. This keeps fresh in our minds the truth that our loving Heavenly Father is always with us and is more powerful than any enemy or circumstance.

Commit to Carrying out the Plan of Action in the Power of the Holy Spirit

Remember, you are never alone in the battle. "It is God who works in you to will and to act according to His good purpose" (Philippians 2:13, NIV).

Fear Finder

Analyse your fear under God's authority and guidance.

Identify all fear objects (i.e. what you are afraid of).

When did you first experience each fear?

What events preceded the first experience?

What are the lies behind every fear?

Determine the ways you have been living under the control of fear rather than living by faith in God.

How has fear:

• Prevented you from doing what is right and responsible?

- Compelled you to do what is wrong and irresponsible?

- Prompted you to compromise your witness for Christ?

Confess any active or passive way in which you have allowed fear to control your life.

Commit yourself to God to live a righteous and responsible life.

Prayerfully work out a plan of responsible behaviour.

Determine in advance what your response will be to any fear object.

Commit yourself to carry out the plan of action in the power of the Holy Spirit.

Appendix C – Seeking the Forgiveness of Others

The Motivation for Seeking Forgiveness

Matthew 5:23–26 is the key passage on seeking forgiveness. Several points in these verses bear emphasising. The worshipper coming before God to offer a gift remembers that someone has something against him. The Holy Spirit is the one who brings to his or her mind the wrong that was done.

Only the actions which have hurt another person need to be confessed to them. If you have had jealous, lustful or angry thoughts towards another, and they don't know about them, these are to be confessed to God alone.

An exception to this principle occurs when restitution needs to be made. If you stole or broke something, damaged someone's reputation, and so on, you need to go to that person and make it right, even if he or she is unaware of what you did.

The Process of Seeking Forgiveness

1. Write out what you did wrong and why you did it.

2. Make sure you have already forgiven the person for whatever they may have done to you.

3. Think through exactly how you will ask them to forgive you. Be sure to:

   a. Label your action as "wrong".

b. Be specific and admit what you did.

c. Make no defences or excuses.

d. Do not blame the other person, and do not expect or demand that they ask for your forgiveness.

e. Your confession should lead to the direct question: "Will you forgive me?"

4. Seek the right place and the right time to approach the offended person.

5. Ask for forgiveness in person from anyone with whom you can talk face-to-face but with the following exception: *do not* go alone when your safety is in danger.

6. Except where no other means of communication is possible, *do not* write a letter because: a letter can be very easily misread or misunderstood; a letter can be read by the wrong people (those having nothing to do with the offence or the confession); a letter can be kept when it should have been destroyed.

7. Once you sincerely seek forgiveness, you are free – whether the other person forgives you or not (see Romans 12:18).

8. After forgiveness, have fellowship with God in worship (see Matthew 5:24).

Appendix D – Forgiving Ourselves And Forgiving God

In Step 3, we are encouraged to recognise that we may need to forgive ourselves and forgive God (even though He has done nothing wrong).

You can use the prayers in Step 3 to do this. Some may, however, prefer to use the prayers below.

Forgiving yourself amounts to the same thing as recognising that you have already been forgiven for what you did or failed to do. Pray as follows:

Lord, I do believe that You have forgiven me and cleansed me of those sins which I have confessed to You. Because of Your great love and grace – not because I deserve it – I choose no longer to condemn myself since You have already forgiven me. I receive Your forgiveness, in Jesus' name. Amen.

When you forgive God, you recognise that He has done nothing wrong but you are being honest about how you felt:

Lord, I release You from my unfulfilled expectations, the grudges I have held against You, and the secret anger and bitterness I have held against You. I choose to believe that You love me and that you want to give me good things. In Jesus' name I pray. Amen. (See Matthew 7:9–11).

Section For Church Leaders

Discipling The Whole Church

Jesus commanded us to "go and make disciples". But, although we may have made some *converts*, most will agree that we have made very few real *disciples*. Far too many ordinary Christians struggle to take hold of basic biblical truth and *live it out*.

Even "good" Christians often take a painfully long time to mature. Others are "stuck" to the negative effects of the past. Still others simply go round and round in cycles of spiritual confusion and habitual sin.

It's not as if we lack excellent discipleship programmes or resources. It's more to do with people's ability to "connect" with truth. Or, as Jesus put it, "You will *know* the truth and the truth shall set you free" (Jn. 8:32, emphasis added).

Freedom In Christ Ministries exists to provide church leaders with everything they need to help people resolve completely the negative effects of the past and take hold of truth, including training in the biblical principles of discipleship and the tools to implement those principles.

The Freedom In Christ Discipleship Course has been used by over 3,000 churches to help well over 125,000 people. Freedom In Christ For Young People is an equivalent course for 11 to 18 year olds. There are also additional resources and training available.

The main resources available are summarised over the next few pages and further details are available from Freedom In Christ Ministries or at www.ficm.org.uk. First, take a look at what leaders who have used them say:

Increasingly, new Christians are carrying huge amounts of spiritual baggage, hurts and strongholds. Traditional discipleship material focusing on growth, gifts and giving was not getting through. We have seen folk suddenly propelled forward at a rate unseen before. This is a very balanced, biblically-based, well-presented course that God is using powerfully.
Sam Griffiths, Wellington Baptist Church, Somerset

The comments most often received from individuals are: "I wish I had known this when I first became a Christian"; "The teaching is so easy to understand"; "No one has ever explained things this way before."
Sandra Stark, Whitlawburn & Springhall Community Church, Glasgow

This has been an excellent resource in our inner city Anglican church where many Christians, young and old, come with heavy loads of emotional baggage. Watching people being set free by the Holy Spirit has been immensely rewarding.
Revd Arani, Senior Vicar, Emmanuel Church, Southall

It has been a joy to watch the amazing transformation in people's lives week by week. We have seen more transformations in three years of running the course than in many years previously. It is an excellent follow-on to Alpha.
Jenny Walker, Head of Discipleship, Tankerton Evangelical Church, Whitstable

A very liberating course that deals with life's issues in a very practical and sensitive way. Our church has been greatly blessed.
Billy Fenning, Senior Leader, St Saviour's Elim Church, Reading

Those of us who have received the teaching and had a Freedom Appointment have been changed by the profound nature of the teaching of God's Word on who we are in Christ, and what this means for us and the Church. We have experienced personal freedom as "the truth" has literally set us free. We highly recommend FIC to churches looking for a teaching of the Gospel that will disciple and change the hearts of church members, so that they are free to look outwards to others and help build God's Kingdom.
Aidan Tod, St Josephs Roman Catholic Church, Guildford

The course has had a dramatic effect on the life of the church. There is a huge new wave of love, compassion and encouragement amongst us. There is a vibrant buzz of expectation of Jesus' healing and restoration.
Liz Smith, All Saints Church, Burbage

The Freedom In Christ Discipleship Course has made a big difference to our church. It is now a significant part of our nurturing of new Christians and we try and build the Discipleship Course into small group life as much as we can. One of the strengths of Freedom In Christ materials is that they are based on the fundamental fact that most Christians' behavioural problems are at root belief problems. As the truth is brought to individuals and they believe it, they become free.
John Groves, Senior Pastor, Winchester Family Church

Like Alpha, the material is not new but is good old-fashioned Christianity. What Neil Anderson and Steve Goss have done is to package it in a very accessible and usable way. With a little training and forethought, anyone in the church can pick up the material and use it. The sup-

port and encouragement from the Freedom In Christ team is outstanding.
Nick Cooper, Pastor, Frome Baptist Church

Our people have been encouraged and motivated to move up a gear. Many shared that they feel somehow "different" and are experiencing a deeper sense of inward freedom. It has brought unity into our Church like never before.
Elizabeth Byrne, Hacketstown Christian Centre, Co. Carlow, Ireland

We have seen a tremendous level of spiritual growth and liberty. Our youth are the majority in our FIC meeting. They come, they want to stay, we can't get them out of church after the service finishes because – Hallelujah! – in Christ they are free.
Sadie Lindsay-Brooks, Local Youth & Christian Education Director, Oldbury New Testament Church of God, Sandwell

We consider the FIC course to be the best material on the market to build Christians up in their walk with Jesus. It encourages personal responsibility and helps people to go deeper with God and discover His blessings. The impact on our church and community has been enormous.
Adrian Pike, Beacon Church, Camberley

The Freedom In Christ Discipleship Course

Equip every Christian to reach their full potential in Christ!

This 13 week course covers Freedom In Christ's basic discipleship teaching in a clear, straightforward style. It's an easy and effective way for any church to implement effective discipleship. It is frequently used as a follow-up to Alpha, Christianity Explored and other introductory courses and has an optional introductory session to provide a bridge from them. Many churches run it two or three times a year as part of their ongoing discipleship activities.

Created specifically for the UK Church, the course can help *every* Christian take hold of the truth of who they are in Christ, resolve personal and spiritual conflicts and become a fruitful disciple.

Either present it yourself or use video presentations available on DVD which include helpful testimonies to illustrate key points.

It works best in small groups but also lends itself to a Sunday teaching series.

Why does it work so well?

Traditional discipleship teaching can easily end up sounding like this: "*do* this every day", "don't *do* that any more", "successful Christians *behave* like this". So Christians end up simply trying to *act* like they think Christians should act. Some manage to do and say the right things but don't necessarily live fruitful lives. Others constantly require help with the same old issues. Some just drift away.

Read any of Paul's letters and you'll get half way through before you find instructions on how to behave.

First he concentrates on what's already been done; the "riches" we have in Christ (Ephesians 1:18). Because it's not what we *do* that determines who we are – it's who we *are* that determines what we do.

The Freedom In Christ course focuses on that too: who we are in Christ; the truth of God's unconditional love; why there is no condemnation; why we don't have to languish in cycles of sin, negative thinking and hopelessness.

But good teaching on its own is not enough. Although the key to freedom is knowing the truth (John 8:32), simply *telling* people the truth doesn't mean that they really *know* it. The course also includes a kind and gentle process called The Steps To Freedom In Christ to help participants repent of past sin and resist the devil. For many this "clearing out of rubbish" is the key to the teaching falling into place.

More details at www.ficm.org.uk

Freedom In Christ For Young People

"Every young disciple is looking to engage with Jesus in a way that will change lives. This innovative, exciting course will help young people discover the truth of who they are in Christ and be set free to be all that God has made them as a result."
Mike Pilavachi, Founder & Director of Soul Survivor

"Freedom In Christ is a creative and relevant course for teenagers with the potential to produce a generation of fruitful young disciples."
Martin Saunders, Editor of Youthwork *Magazine*

The aim of Freedom In Christ For Young People is to set young people firmly on the way to becoming fruitful disciples who are sold out for God and will make a radical difference. Watch them change as they connect with the truth about who they are in Christ, become free from pressures that hold them back and learn to renew their thinking – no matter what their circumstances or background.

The course is based on the main Freedom In Christ course and can be run alongside it. The sessions correspond exactly (including the optional introductory session). It was created in the UK by a team from British Youth For Christ and Freedom In Christ Ministries.

The emphasis is on relevant, interactive, multi-media based material tailored to meet the needs of 11–18 year olds. It is split into two age ranges, 11–14 and 15–18. Each session is packed full of age-appropriate games, activities, discussion-starters, film clip suggestions and talk slots.

There is also a video teaching component for each session. Presented by Nathan Iles and Kate John from Youth For Christ, the video material was shot entirely on location and is punchy, contemporary and entertaining. It gets the main points across in segments of just two to four minutes (with around three segments per session).

For more details go to: www.ficm.org.uk/youth

Training Your Team

Freedom In Christ holds a number of equipping events around the UK on a regular basis. There are three core events that will be of particular interest to anyone involved in leading the Freedom In Christ course. Ideally they should be attended in the order listed below.

Getting Started With Freedom In Christ

Aimed at church leaders and youth leaders, this event gives an overview of the theological principles behind the Freedom In Christ approach and then shows you practically how to get started with the Freedom In Christ and Freedom In Christ For Young People courses. Anyone planning to lead a Freedom In Christ course will benefit from it. (See also the Making Fruitful Disciples DVD training course below).

Helping Others Find Freedom In Christ

This event focuses on The Steps To Freedom In Christ and its objective is to help participants feel confident about using the Steps to lead others to freedom. It is ideal for churches who are using the Freedom In Christ Discipleship course or Freedom In Christ For Young People. It will equip you to lead the Steps in individual appointments or on an away day. (For the corresponding DVD course see below.)

Helping Others With Deeper Issues

The Freedom In Christ course is for every Christian but the principles in it can be applied highly effectively to those struggling with deeper issues such as past abuse, addictions and dissociative disorders. God does not change our past but He promises to set us free from it. This workshop is for those who are already familiar with the basic Freedom In Christ approach and is ideal for church teams.

Training On DVD

It is not always possible for everyone to attend a 'live' event so the content of our two main equipping events are available on DVD making it easy to train a team in your church.

Making Fruitful Disciples

Don't settle for making converts – make fruitful disciples! An outline of the key biblical principles for helping people mature as Christians and practical ways to implement them in your church using the Freedom In Christ course and Freedom In Christ For Young People.

Helping Others Find Freedom In Christ

How to help every Christian walk in freedom. This DVD is a practical guide to using The Steps To Freedom In Christ to lead both individual appointments and away days.

Further details are available at www.ficm.org.uk.

Taking The Principles Further

The same biblical principles that are taught on the Freedom In Christ course have wider applications. Once you are up and running, you may want to look at using them in some of these areas:

Resolving Deeper Issues

Freedom In Christ has two main messages. The first is that every Christian will benefit from taking hold of what Christ has given them and resolving personal and spiritual conflicts in order to become a fruitful disciple. The second is that no Christian is too "messed up" or has problems that are too deep that through Christ they cannot resolve those issues (not just develop ways of coping) and become fruitful disciples.

We have training and resources that will equip your church to help Christians who are struggling with deeper issues such as past abuse, eating disorders, depression, fear, addiction, self-harm, trauma or dissociative identity disorder. We want to encourage you by assuring you that these people are not 'hopeless cases' but really can become fruitful disciples. We have seen it happen many times in ordinary churches as ordinary people do extraordinary things through Christ. The role of Freedom In Christ Ministries is to encourage and advise you as you, together with your church family, lead hurting people to freedom.

Setting Your Marriage Free

Taking hold of personal freedom is one thing. Couples can also choose to take hold of corporate freedom in their marriage by going through a process similar to The Steps To Freedom In Christ together. It makes good marriages better and can sometimes lead to dramatic improvements in struggling marriages. Freedom In Christ runs regular "Setting Your Marriage Free" retreats for couples in church leadership. Come for your own marriage and also to learn how to take it back to your church using our resources for marriage.

Setting Your Church Free

Churches can get stuck in patterns of division, strife and recurring sin. Good teaching and good mediation do not always resolve the issues. It's easy to look inwards and assume that "other people" are the problem. But that is to ignore the spiritual reality. We are not fighting people but "spiritual forces of wickedness". We ignore that truth at our peril. It is entirely possible to give the enemy ground in the corporate structure of our churches or simply to leave in place footholds given to him in the past. Resolving those corporate footholds is not difficult and often leads to dramatic changes.

Setting Your Church Free is a corporate retreat for church leadership teams during which they are equipped to resolve negative patterns, division, recurring sin, control and entrenched issues.

Setting Your Community Free

Freedom In Christ Ministries has started to work with groups of leaders around the country to apply the approach used in Setting Your Church Free to the one Church in an area. Where there is true unity and leaders come together in genuine repentance for any unresolved corporate sins of the Church, we expect to see breakthroughs in the spiritual environment with the result that many more people become Christians. We are available to act as catalysts and encouragers to groups of leaders who regularly have fellowship together.

For more information on any of these areas, please consult our website at www.ficm.org.uk or call us on 0118 321 8084.

The Freedom In Christ Discipleship Series

You will benefit significantly more from *The Steps To Freedom In Christ* if you also go through the accompanying teaching material. If you are unable to attend a Freedom In Christ course in your church, this series of four slim, easy-to-digest books by Steve Goss is the next best thing. They cost £5.99 each or £19.95 for all four (plus £3 p&p). Available from Christian bookshops or from Freedom In Christ at www.ficm.org.uk or by calling 0118 321 8084.

Free to be Yourself — Enjoy your true nature in Christ.
Many Christians act as they think a Christian should act — and find that they simply can't keep it up. They either drop out or burn out. True fruitfulness comes from realising that we became someone completely new the moment we became Christians.

Win the Daily Battle — Resist and stand firm.
You are in a raging battle, whether you like it or not. Your only choice is to stand and fight or to become a casualty. Arrayed against you are the world, the devil and the flesh but once you understand how they work and just who you are in Christ, you can expect to emerge victorious from every skirmish with them.

Break Free, Stay Free — Don't let the past hold you back.
Every Christian has a past. It can hold us back big-time. Those of us with a lot of "stuff" know that only too well. But even those who have had a relatively trouble-free existence need to know how to resolve negative influences that stop us moving on.

The You God Planned — Don't let anything hold you back!
Once we have claimed our freedom in Christ, how do we remain in it and make fruitfulness a way of life? How do we know what God is calling us to be anyway? Are the goals we have for our lives in line with His goals? How can we stop others getting in the way? And how do we avoid getting in their way?